S0-BYF-304

Alfred's
Teach Yourself
To Play Mandolin

DAN FOX

Everything you need to know to start playing now!

 ON AVAILABLE DVD

In addition to video lessons, the companion DVD includes Alfred's exclusive TNT 2 software which allows users to customize the audio tracks in this book for practice. Use it to slow down tracks, isolate and loop parts, and change tempos and keys.

To install, insert the DVD into the disc drive of your computer.

Windows
Double-click on **My Computer**, right-click on the DVD drive icon, and select **Explore**. Open the **DVD-ROM Materials** folder, then the **TnT2** folder, then the **Windows** folder, and double-click on the installer file.

Macintosh
Double-click on the DVD icon on your desktop. Open the **DVD-ROM Materials** folder, then the **TnT2** folder, then the **Mac** folder, and double-click on the installer file.

TNT 2 SYSTEM REQUIREMENTS

Windows
XP, Vista, 7, 8
QuickTime 7.6.7 or higher
1.8 GHz processor or faster
900 MB hard drive space
2 GB RAM minimum
DVD drive for installation
Speakers or headphones
Internet access for updates

Macintosh
OS 10.4 and higher (Intel only)
QuickTime 7.6.7 or higher
900 MB hard drive space
2 GB RAM minimum
DVD drive for installation
Speakers or headphones
Internet access for updates

Alfred

Alfred Music
P.O. Box 10003
Van Nuys, CA 91410-0003
alfred.com

ISBN-10: 0-7390-0286-4 (Book only)
ISBN-13: 978-0-7390-0286-5 (Book only)
ISBN-10: 1-4706-1498-7 (Book & CD & DVD)
ISBN-13: 978-1-4706-1498-0 (Book & CD & DVD)

Audio recording by Greg Horne

 Alfred Cares. Contents printed on environmentally responsible paper.

CONTENTS

A SHORT HISTORY OF THE MANDOLIN

The modern mandolin developed from an earlier family of lute-like fretted instruments called mandores. Although at first there were several different types of mandolins, some having as many as eight sets of double strings, the one that is universally used today for Italian, bluegrass and classical music is the Neapolitan mandolin. This instrument can have either a flat back with *f*-holes (preferred by bluegrass players) or a rounded back with a round hole (preferred by those who enjoy playing Italian songs). Classical players are divided in their choices.

The mandolin has four double sets of strings, each attached to its own tuning peg. The strings are attached to a tailpiece, cross over a bridge, and then stretch over a fingerboard that usually contains 20 frets. Markers (sometimes mother-of-pearl) are set into the fingerboard to help the player find a particular fret. These markers are usually at the 3rd, 5th, 7th, 10th, 12th and 15th frets.

The mandolin was developed in Italy in the early part of the 18th century. Vivaldi's concerto for the instrument, which dates from this time, was the main theme of the 1979 film *Kramer vs. Kramer*. Although the concerto had been little known until this time, its use in the film made it popular and stirred up renewed interest in the mandolin as a classical instrument. Other composers who wrote for the mandolin include Handel, Grétry, Paesiello (who used it in his *Barber of Seville* and also wrote a concerto for it), Mozart (*Don Giovanni*), Beethoven (Five pieces for mandolin and piano), Verdi (*Otello*), Mahler (*Das Lied von der Erde*), and Schoenberg (*Serenade*).

Today there are many all-mandolin orchestras which use mandolins to play the violin parts, mandolas for the viola parts, mando-cellos for cello parts, and mando-basses for the bass parts. These orchestras play everything from symphonies to show tunes.

The popularity of the mandolin as a classical instrument and as an instrument on which to play folk songs is easily understood, but no one could have predicted how the mandolin has become such an important part of country music.

The bluegrass phenomenon started in the late 1920s with Bill Monroe, continued through the virtuosic Flatt and Scruggs, and today encompasses hundreds of groups usually featuring a mandolin, five-string banjo, fiddle, guitar and bass. There are dozens of great bluegrass mandolin players today bringing the instrument to new heights of virtuosity.

In this book you'll receive a thorough grounding in the basics of mandolin playing. Whether your interest is classical, folk, alternative rock, bluegrass or even jazz, the fundamentals of playing the instrument are the same. After completion of *Teach Yourself to Play Mandolin* you'll be ready to excel in whatever music you're interested in.

GETTING STARTED THE MANDOLIN

Note: The mandolin pictured here is a flat back model with *f*-holes. Your model may have a rounded, bowl-shaped back and a round sound hole, but the rest of the parts are the same.

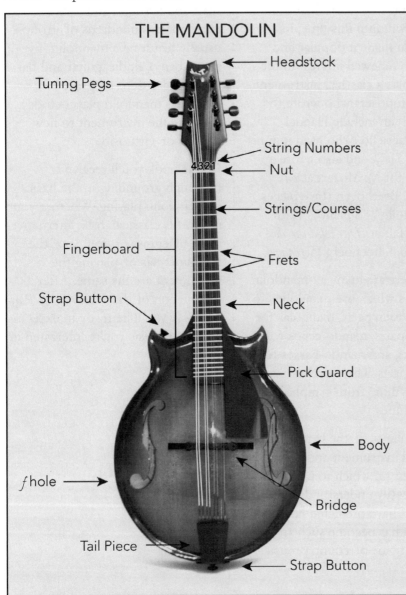

THE MANDOLIN

- Headstock
- Tuning Pegs
- String Numbers
- 4321
- Nut
- Strings/Courses
- Fingerboard
- Frets
- Strap Button
- Neck
- Pick Guard
- Body
- *f* hole
- Bridge
- Tail Piece
- Strap Button

NOTE: Some mandolins include a pickup, which is a device that allows you to amplify the instrument. The pickup transmits the vibrations from the bridge of the mandolin through a cable to an amplifier. Because the mandolin isn't a very loud instrument, a pickup and amplifier is necessary when playing in ensembles that feature louder instruments, such as a banjo or electric guitar. However, all classical and folk players, and most Italian music aficionados, prefer the sound of the unamplified or acoustic mandolin.

PICKS

Mandolin is played by striking the strings with a pick held in the right hand. The pick (or plectrum) is a triangular or oval-shaped piece of plastic or tortoise shell which varies in size and flexibility. You should experiment with different types of picks until you find one that feels comfortable (and don't be surprised if your taste changes as you improve on the instrument).

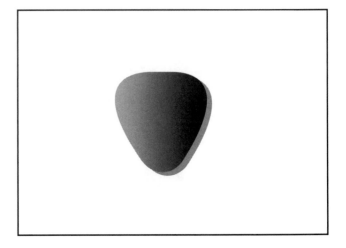

▲ *The pick.*

TUNING YOUR MANDOLIN

The mandolin has eight strings arranged in four pairs. First, make sure that you understand how each string is threaded through a tuning peg. The four on the right are wound clockwise; the four on the left are wound counter-clockwise.

The strings are tightened or loosened by turning the tuning machines on the sides of the head (see drawing above).

• Turning the machine clockwise loosens the string and lowers the pitch.

• Turning the machine counter-clockwise tightens the string and raises the pitch.

TUNING TO A PIANO OR OTHER KEYBOARD

1. Find middle C.

2. Counting middle C as 1, find the 10th white key to the right of it. This note is called E.

3. Tune the 1st string to this note. Tighten or loosen the tuning machine as necessary. Note: The 1st string is the thinnest string (the one furthest to the right as you look at the mandolin with the tuning pegs up).

4. Tune the 2nd string to this note also. The 1st pair of strings should now sound the same.

5. Find middle A on the keyboard. This is the 6th white key to the right of middle C. Tune the 2nd pair of strings to this note.

6. Find middle D on the keyboard. This is the white key next to middle C on the right. Tune the 3rd pair of strings to this note.

7. Find the G below middle C on the keyboard. This is the 4th white key to the left of middle C. Tune the lowest pair of strings to this note.

This completes the tuning procedure using a keyboard.

OTHER WAYS OF TUNING YOUR MANDOLIN

Tuning to a Pitch Pipe

Since the mandolin is tuned like a violin, you can tune it using a violin pitch pipe. Match the 1st or highest pair of strings to E, the 2nd pair to A, the 3rd pair to D and the 4th or lowest pair to G as marked on the pitch pipe.

Tuning to a Tuning Fork

A tuning fork can be used to tune the mandolin. First, make sure that the fork gives the pitch of A = 440 vibrations per second. This will be stamped into the fork itself.

The best way of tuning with a fork is to hold the fork by the stem and strike the tines against any soft surface such as your elbow. (**Never** strike the fork against anything hard such as a table. This will eventually damage the fork.) With the fork still vibrating place it between your back teeth. Bone conduction will let you hear the note A = 440 while leaving both hands free to tune the strings.

Tune the 2nd pair of strings to this note. Once they are in tune, press the 2nd pair of strings at the 7th fret and tune the 1st pair of strings to it. Then press the 3rd pair of strings at the 7th fret and tune them till they sound like the 2nd pair of strings open (not fretted). Finally, press the 4th pair of strings at the 7th fret and tune them till they sound like the 3rd pair open (see diagram at right).

Using an Electronic Tuner

An electronic tuner can be purchased at any music store. They range in quality and price, but some of the low-end models can be bought for $40 or less. The advantages of using an electronic tuner are that it's easy and accurate. But relying solely on an electronic tuner can hinder the need for you to train your ear. Anyone who hopes to play reasonably well must depend on the ear to tell when something is correct or not and, more subtly, to tell whether a tune is being played tastefully or not.

Suggestion: Tune the instrument using one of the methods described above. Then check the tuning using the electronic tuner.

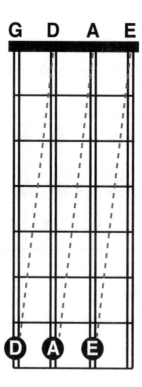

Caring for your Mandolin

Strings should be wiped with a soft rag after each session of playing the mandolin. Otherwise, they may corrode from the dampness and lose their brilliance. With ordinary usage, strings should last up to a year. After that, replace the strings with a new set. It's best to ask your local music store repair person how to do this.

If you decide to do it yourself, replace one string at a time and bring each new string up to pitch before replacing the next one. This is important! If you remove all the strings at once, the bridge will slip out of place, and it is no small job to reset it correctly.

Once in a while wipe the body and neck of the mandolin with a light polish such as guitar polish. This will not only keep the instrument looking nice, but will protect the surfaces against dust and dirt.

About every six months put a tiny drop of sewing machine oil (or some other very light oil) in the tuning gears.

Above all, do not allow the mandolin to be exposed to extremes of heat or cold. Either one may crack the body. Although cracks can be repaired, each one takes away from the beauty of the tone.

When not being played, store the mandolin in its case. Always use the case when carrying the instrument from place to place.

Used Mandolins

Since a good-quality new mandolin can cost around $400 or more (first-rate top-of-the-line ones can cost thousands of dollars), you may consider buying a used instrument. If you do, look for the following when shopping for a good used one:

1. Is the neck straight? (Look for bowing from end to end or twisting from side to side.)

2. Can the tuning gears be turned fairly easily? (They may only need a little oil. But if they are bent or rusted, be prepared to replace them at a cost of up to $100.)

3. Is the instrument crack free? (Small cracks are usually easy to fix, but a neck that has been broken and then repaired is good reason not to buy the instrument.)

4. Is the action fairly easy? (The word "action" refers to how high off the fingerboard the strings are. You should be able to slide a shirt cardboard between the strings and the fingerboard, but if the strings are any further away than this they will be difficult to push down and will hurt your fingers. Any competent repair person will be able to adjust the action if the instrument has nothing else wrong with it.)

If you can answer yes to the four questions above, the instrument is probably worth buying.

STARTING TO PLAY

The mandolin is held in the lap. You may also cross your left leg over the right if it feels more comfortable to you.

▲ *Holding the mandolin*

The pick is held firmly in the right hand. The strings are struck with a downward sweep of the wrist, not the entire arm.

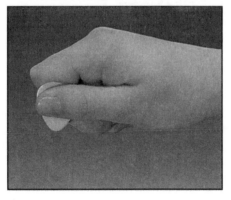

▲ *How to hold the pick.*

Exercise No. 1

Strike the lowest double strings 16 times. Keep a steady beat about as fast as a march and be aware of how loud you're playing. Notice that the sound becomes louder as you strike the strings harder.

Repeat using the next double strings. Start soft and get louder. Then start loud and get softer.

Repeat using the next double strings.

Finally, repeat the exercise using the highest (thinnest) double strings.

GETTING ACQUAINTED WITH MUSIC

Notes are the basic units of music. They tell you two things: what pitch to play (melody) and how long to play it (rhythm). There are several types of notes—open, open with stems, closed with stems, and closed with stems and flags (see diagram 1).

Written music tells you what pitch to play by placing notes on a five-line **staff** (see diagram 2). The notes are named by letters: A B C D E F G. No other letters are used.

In order to identify the notes on the five-line staff, a symbol called a **clef** is placed at the beginning of each staff. Music for the mandolin is written in the **treble clef**. The treble clef symbol is derived from the Gothic letter G:

The modern clef still shows the position of the note G by curling around the second line of the staff, the place where G is written.

Bar lines are vertical lines that divide the staff into **measures** (see diagram 3). This shows the basic pulse of the music and makes reading music easier by dividing the notes into shorter groups.

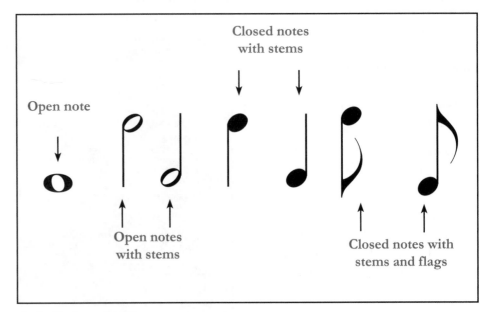

▲ 1. *Various types of notes.*

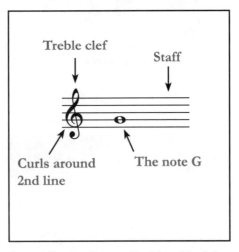

▲ 2. *The five-line staff with treble clef*

▼ 3. *Measures and bar lines.*

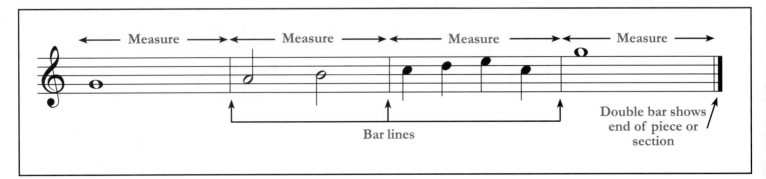

NAMING THE NOTES & RHYTHM

Notes are placed on the five-line staff either in the spaces or on the lines.

Notes in
the spaces
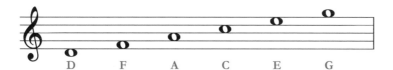

Notes on
the lines
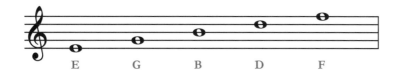

The following memory tricks will help you identify the notes:

In the spaces: **D**on't **F**orget, **A**ll **C**ows **E**at **G**rass

On the lines: **E**very **G**ood **B**oy **D**oes **F**ine

Identify the following notes and write their names in the spaces provided below each staff.
(Check your answers with the two staffs above.)

In the spaces

1.

On the lines

2.

In random order

3.

Rhythm refers to the way notes relate to a steady beat. Try this: Tap your foot to a steady beat like a march. Now play any open string once for each tap of your foot. These notes are called **quarter notes**. They are written as black egg shapes (the **note head**) with stems going either up or down:

Half notes have a duration of two beats. They are written as open

egg shapes with stems going either up or down:

Dotted half notes have a duration of three beats. They are written the same as half notes followed by a dot directly to the right of the note head:

Whole notes have a duration of four beats. They are written as open egg shapes without stems:

o

The notes described above can appear on any line or space of the five-line staff.

• **The position of the note on the staff tells you its name.**

• **The shape of the note tells you its duration.**

Generally speaking, all the notes described above are played with a downstroke of the pick. Later we'll show you other notes that use upstrokes of the pick.

NAMING THE NOTES ON THE 2nd STRING

From now on we will refer to each set of double strings as "the string." (Since the strings in each double set are tuned to the same note, there is no point in continually repeating the expression "double strings.")

The five basic notes on the 2nd string are:

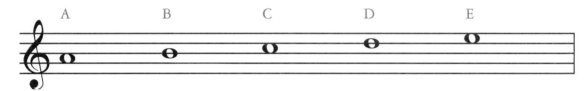

Exercise: Practice naming the notes below.

PLAYING THE NOTES ON THE 2nd STRING

Any note which is not an open string must be fingered. Press the finger down on the string directly behind, not on, the fret. Then strike the string with a downstroke of the pick. Although you're actually playing two strings when you do this, the pick stroke should be rapid enough so that you hear only one sound.

The tone should be clear and bell-like. If it's not, make sure you're not:

• pressing down too lightly on the string

• pressing too far from the fret (you should be pressing slightly behind the fret, not directly over it.)

The photos show the placement of the fingers for the notes on the 2nd string.

A
Open (no fingers)

B
1st finger, 2nd fret

C
2nd finger, 3rd fret

D
3rd finger, 5th fret

E
4th finger, 7th fret

These exercises use only the notes on the A string (the 2nd string). Count carefully and work on getting a clear, bell-like tone. Use only downstrokes of the pick.

Track 2

Exercise with whole notes

Count: 1   2   3   4   1   2   3   4   1   2   3   4   1   2   3   4   1   2   3   4

Track 3

Exercise with half notes

Count: 1   2   3   4   1   2   3   4   1   2   3   4   1   2   3   4   1   2   3   4

Track 4

Exercise with quarter notes

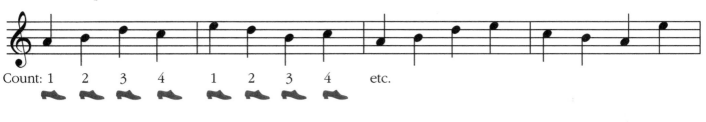

Count: 1   2   3   4   1   2   3   4   etc.

 MINI MUSIC LESSON # TIME SIGNATURES

These exercises use a count of four as their basic rhythm. In music this is called $\frac{4}{4}$ time (say "four-quarter time" or "four-four"). The following exercise uses a basic count of three. This is called $\frac{3}{4}$ ("three-quarter" or "three-four") time. $\frac{4}{4}$ and $\frac{3}{4}$ are called **time signatures**. The time signature appears once at the beginning of every piece.

Track 5

Exercise with dotted half notes

Time Signature

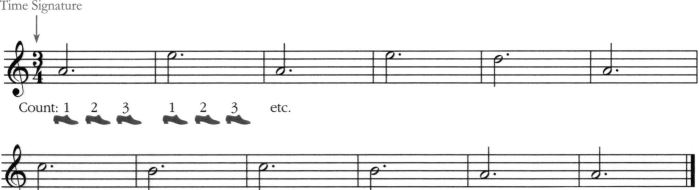

Count: 1   2   3   1   2   3   etc.

NAMING THE NOTES ON THE 3rd STRING

The five basic notes on the 3rd string are:

Notice that the last note on the 3rd string is the same as the 2nd string open. The only difference between them is that the A on the 3rd string must be fingered, while the A on the 2nd string is played open. Later you'll find that this is an advantage that makes fingering certain passages easier. In this book we'll label the note with an "o" for the open-string A and with a 4 for the fingered A. If no fingering is indicated, play the note open.

Exercise: Practice naming the notes below. Then cover the staff above and continue naming the notes till you can do this fairly easily.

PLAYING THE NOTES ON THE 3rd STRING

The photos show the placement of the fingers for the notes on the 3rd string. Remember to press hard directly behind, not on, the fret.

D
Open (no fingers)

E
1st finger, 2nd fret

F
2nd finger, 3rd fret

G
3rd finger, 5th fret

A
4th finger, 7th fret

The following exercises use only the notes on the 3rd string. Count carefully and strive for a clean tone.

Exercise with whole notes

Count: 1 2 3 4   1 2 3 4   etc.

Exercise with half notes

Count: 1 2 3 4   1 2 3 4   etc.

Exercise with dotted half notes

Count: 1 2 3   1 2 3   etc.

Exercise with quarter notes

Count: 1   2   3   4   1   2   3   4   etc.

This next exercise uses all of the notes on the 3rd and 2nd strings shown to you so far. When you see the note A with an "o" above it, play it on the 2nd string open. When the note A has a 4 above it, play it on the 3rd string, 7th fret.

JUST FOR FUN

Here are three well-known songs to play. Each one makes use of notes on the 2nd and 3rd strings as well as whole, dotted half, half and quarter notes. Again, count carefully and strive for a clean tone.

RESTS

When silence is called for in music, a symbol called a **rest** is used. It is important to remember that a rest is a **measured silence**, that is, a silence that lasts for a certain number of beats.

A **quarter rest** looks like this ⌀. The quarter rest represents one beat of silence. When a fingered note is followed by a rest, release the pressure on the string but keep the finger touching it to stop the vibration of the string.

Finger   Release   Finger   Release

When an open note is followed by a rest, lightly lay any left hand finger on the string to stop its vibration.

Play open string   Lay any left hand finger lightly on string   Play open string   Lay any left hand finger lightly on string

The **half rest** represents two beats of silence. It looks like a short, thick dash resting on the 3rd line of the staff:

It only appears in 4/4 time either on the 1st or 3rd beat of the measure (never the 2nd!).

Track 14

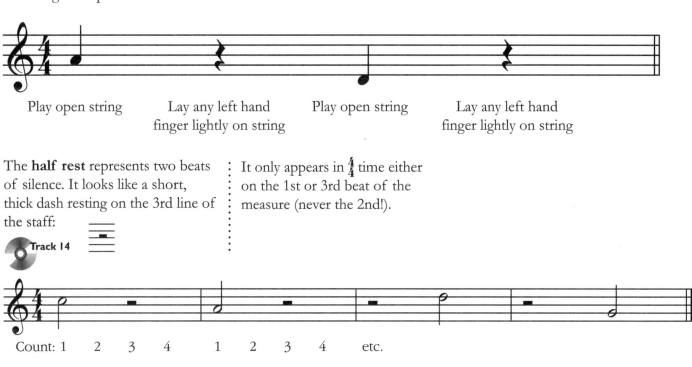

Count: 1   2   3   4   1   2   3   4   etc.

The **whole rest** represents a whole measure of silence. In 4/4 the whole rest gets four beats of silence. In 3/4 it gets three beats of silence. The

whole rest looks like a short, thick dash hanging from the 4th line of the staff:

Track 15

Count: 1   2   3   4   1   2   3   4   etc.

Track 16

Count: 1   2   3   1   2   3   etc.

NAMING THE NOTES ON THE 1st STRING

Since the mandolin can play notes higher than those written on the staff, it is sometimes necessary to extend the five lines of the staff with short, temporary lines called **leger lines**. Leger lines are used to notate the high A and B which are played on the 1st string, the E string.

The five basic notes on the 1st string are:

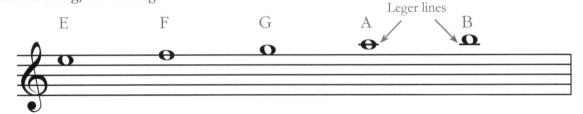

Notice the use of the leger lines for the notes A and B. Also notice that the note E, which is played open on the 1st string, can also be played on the 2nd string 7th fret. The fingering number above the note will tell you whether to play it open ("o") or fingered (4).

Exercise: Practice naming the notes below.

PLAYING THE NOTES ON THE 1st STRING

These photos show the proper placement of the fingers for the notes on the 1st string. Remember to press hard directly behind the fret.

Important! Unlike the 2nd and 3rd strings, the 1st finger plays the note on the 1st (not the 2nd) fret.

E
Open (no fingers)

F
1st finger, 1st fret

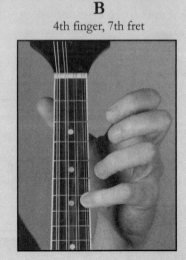

G
2nd finger, 3rd fret

A
3rd finger, 5th fret

B
4th finger, 7th fret

The following exercise uses only the notes on the 1st string. Make sure you can play it confidently and with a good, clean tone before continuing.

Track 17

This next exercise uses only the notes on the 1st and 2nd strings. The fingering number above the note E tells you whether to play it open on the 1st string or on the 2nd string, 7th fret.

Track 18

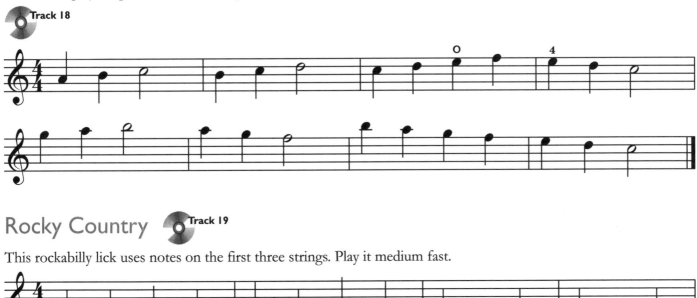

Rocky Country   **Track 19**

This rockabilly lick uses notes on the first three strings. Play it medium fast.

NAMING THE NOTES ON THE 4th STRING

Since the mandolin can play notes that are lower than those on the staff, leger lines are used to extend the staff downward.

The five basic notes on the 4th string are

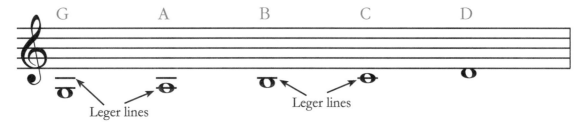

Notice the use of leger lines for the notes G, A, B and C. Also notice that the note D, which is played on the 4th string, 7th fret is the same note as the 3rd string open. Look for the number above the D for the proper fingering.

Exercise: Practice naming the notes on the G string below.

PLAYING THE NOTES ON THE 4th STRING

The photos show the placement of the fingers for the notes on the 4th string.

G
Open (no fingers)

A
1st finger, 2nd fret

B
2nd finger, 4th fret

C
3rd finger, 5th fret

D
4th finger, 7th fret

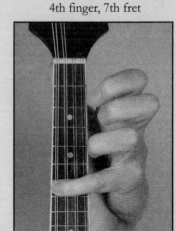

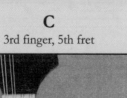

Track 20

This exercise uses only notes found on the G (or 4th) string.

Track 21

This exercise uses notes found on the G and D (3rd) strings.

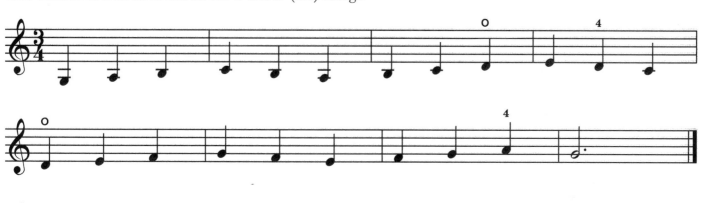

Track 22

This exercise makes use of all the notes you've learned so far.

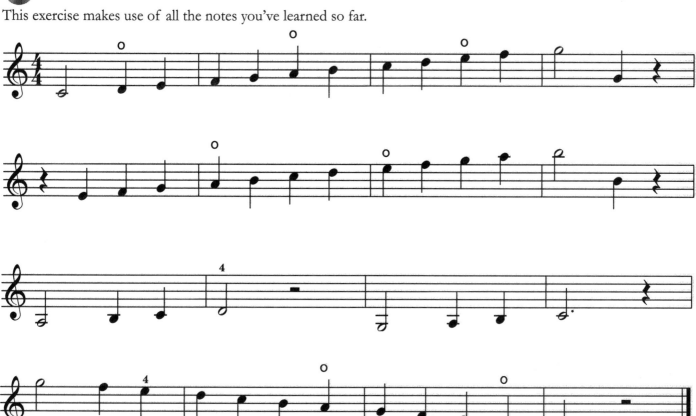

MINI MUSIC LESSON PICKUPS

Sometimes a song or other piece of music begins with an incomplete measure called a **pickup**. In $\frac{4}{4}$ time the pickup can be one, two or three beats. (Later you'll learn that pickups can even use fractional beats.) In $\frac{3}{4}$ time the pickup can be one or two beats. Often the last measure of the song will be missing the same number of beats that the pickup uses. For example, if in $\frac{4}{4}$ time there is a one beat pickup, the last measure may have three beats. In this way the initial incomplete measure is completed.

Here are some short excerpts of familiar tunes showing pickups of various numbers of beats in $\frac{4}{4}$ and $\frac{3}{4}$ time.

Jimmy Crack Corn (one beat pickup in $\frac{4}{4}$)   Track 23

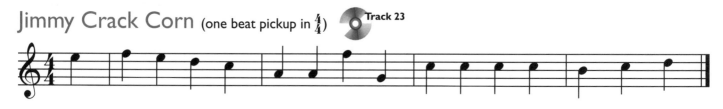

Red River Valley (two beat pickup in $\frac{4}{4}$)

From this val - ley they sat you are go - ing . . .

Oh Happy Day (three beat pickup in $\frac{4}{4}$)

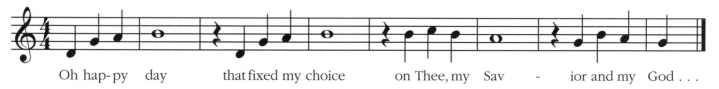

Oh hap-py day   that fixed my choice   on Thee, my Sav - ior and my God . . .

The Beautiful Blue Danube (one beat pickup in $\frac{3}{4}$)

Cowboy Jack (two beat pickup in $\frac{3}{4}$)

He was just a lone - ly cow - boy . . .

 ## THE TIE

The tie is a curved line that connects two or more notes of the same pitch. When two notes are tied, the second note is not played separately but its value is added to the first note. For example, two tied whole notes are held for eight beats. A half note tied to a quarter note is held for three beats and so on.

The following songs make use of ties and pickups. Play the songs with a steady beat and good tone.

MINI MUSIC LESSON **THE FERMATA** ⌢

The sign ⌢ is called a fermata. It means to hold the note it is over a little longer (about twice its value).

Reuben, Reuben Track 26

Country song

The Yellow Rose of Texas Track 27

Country song

Here are two famous Italian melodies that are naturals on the mandolin. Chord symbols for optional accompaniment by guitar or accordion are included.

Vieni sul Mar (Come to the Sea) — Track 28

Neapolitan folk song

Ah! Marie — Track 29

Eduardo Di Capua

Eighth Notes

Eighth notes look like ♪ or ♪ when they stand alone. When they are written in groups of two or more they look like this:

Eighth notes are played twice as fast as quarter notes, that is, two for each beat. In $\frac{4}{4}$ count them as 1 & 2 & 3 & 4 &. In $\frac{3}{4}$ count them as 1 & 2 & 3 &.

On the mandolin pairs of eighth notes are usually played with downstrokes and upstrokes. The symbol for a downstroke is ⊓. For an upstroke, we use V.

Make sure you can play the first line accurately before attempting the rest of the page.

Track 30

Exercises Using Eighth Notes

Track 31

No. 1

Track 32

No. 2

Track 33

No. 3

JUST FOR FUN

Buffalo Gals

Track 34

Square dance song

Johann Pachelbel

Canon (Main theme)

Track 35

Can-Can (from Orpheus in the Underworld)

Track 36

Jacques Offenbach

Wildwood Flower

Track 37

Bluegrass standard

THE SHARP ♯

The symbol ♯ is used to indicate a **sharp**. A note with a sharp in front of it is played one fret higher (closer to the bridge). For example, F is played on the 3rd string, 3rd fret; F♯ is played on the 3rd string, 4th fret. On the 1st string F is played on the 1st fret and F♯ on the 2nd fret. Low G is the 4th string open; low G♯ is the 4th string, 1st fret.

The symbol ♮ is a **natural** sign which cancels the sharp and restores the note to the usual pitch. For example, in a single measure, F is played on the 3rd string, 3rd fret; F♯ is played on the 3rd string, 4th fret; F♮ is played on the 3rd string, 3rd fret.

The exercises below show the fingering for every sharp commonly played in the 1st position.

Rockin' the Bach   Track 38

Adapted from a minuet by J.S. Bach

Here are two well known tunes that use sharps. If you have trouble finding any sharped note, refer to the exercises on the previous page.

Old Joe Clarke — Track 39

Square dance tune

Still sharp: sharp affects every C note in this measure

Little Brown Jug (Square dance version) — Track 40

19th century vaudeville tune

THE FLAT ♭

The symbol ♭ is used to indicate a **flat**. A note with a flat in front of it is played one fret lower (closer to the nut) than usual. On the 1st string G is played on the 3rd fret; G♭ is played on the 2nd fret. On the 1st string

2nd string, D is played on the 5th fret; D♭ is played on the 4th fret, and so on.

Open strings cannot be flatted, but the same note can be found with alternate fingering on the next lower string. For example, since

the open E string cannot be flatted, find the E on the 2nd string, 7th fret; E♭ is played on the 2nd string, 6th fret. The exercises below show the fingering for every flat commonly played in the 1st position.

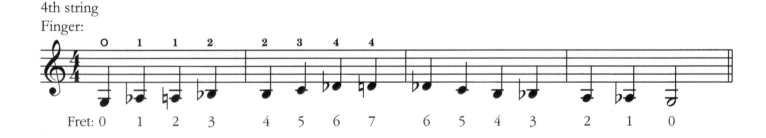

Don't forget that a natural sign (♮) restores a flatted note to its usual pitch. **Flats or sharps affect all the following notes of that pitch in that measure only.** Example:

(Also see fingering chart on page 72)

My Melancholy Baby
A study in flats and naturals

Track 41

George Norton
and Ernie Burnett

TREMOLO

One of the characteristics of the mandolin is its limited ability to sustain a note. For example, in measures 7 and 8 of the previous song, two whole notes are tied. As you may have noticed, the sound of the note dies away long before the end of the tied notes.

About 200 years ago players developed a technique called the tremolo to overcome this deficiency. This consists of rapid and repeated downstrokes and upstrokes. When done properly, the tremolo produces a smooth tone which can be sustained indefinitely. Another advantage is that the tone can be made to get louder or softer by increasing or decreasing the pressure used to produce it.

The tremolo makes use of certain muscles in the right wrist and forearm which must be trained and strengthened. Throughout this book you'll be provided with exercises that will allow you to develop this technique.

Tremolo Exercise No. 1

Start at about a march tempo. (If you have a metronome, set it at 120 beats per minute. We highly recommend purchasing an electronic metronome which can be set at any tempo from about 40 to 240 beats per minute.) Follow the picking very carefully.

Once you can do the exercise at 120, increase the speed by about four beats per minute. Then continue increasing the speed every day until you reach the limit of how fast you can play. This exercise should be practiced every day for at least five to ten minutes.

Keep the wrist loose and relaxed. A stiff wrist and forearm will result in a harsh tone and muscle cramps.

Track 42

When to Use Tremolo

Choosing when to use tremolo is largely a matter of taste. In classical music at a slow to moderate tempo any note longer than an eighth note may be played with tremolo. At faster tempos only half notes and longer should be tremoloed. Tremolo is always appropriate in Italian music, but is less used in bluegrass. Knowledgeable composers and arrangers do not leave this up to chance, but indicate where they want a tremolo by placing three cross bars through the stem of a note with the abbreviation *trem.* above it.

Track 43

In this famous Neapolitan melody we have suggested where to use tremolo. However, don't hesitate to add more if you wish.

O Sole Mio

Track 44

Eduardo Di Capua

THREE MAJOR SCALES

A **major scale** is a succession of eight notes in alphabetical order. For example, the C major scale consists of the notes C D E F G A B C. Notice that the first and last notes have the same name.

Another characteristic of major scales is that they consist of a certain pattern of whole steps and half steps. On the mandolin a **half step** is one fret. For example, from E (1st string open) to F (1st string, 1st fret) is a half step; from that F to F♯ (1st string, 2nd fret) is also a half step and so on. A **whole step** is two frets or two half steps. For example, from E (1st string open) to F♯ (1st string, 2nd fret) is a whole step. From F (1st string, 1st fret) to G (1st string, 3rd fret) is a whole step, and so on.

For a scale to be called a major scale, the pattern of steps must be:

whole step, whole step, half step, **whole step, whole step, whole step,** half step.

Here's how it works out in the scale of C major:

The C Major Scale

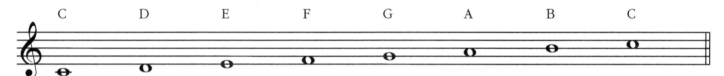

If we start on G, one sharp must be used to make the notes conform to the major scale pattern. The note F must be played as F♯.

The G Major Scale

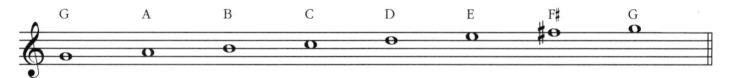

If we start on D, two sharps must be used to make the notes conform to the major scale pattern. The notes F and C must be played as F♯ and C♯.

The D Major Scale

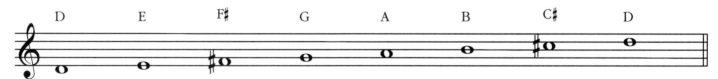

KEY SIGNATURES

A piece of music based on the G major scale is said to be in the **key of G**. Musicians use a shortcut to indicate the key of a piece called a **key signature**. As you have seen on the previous page, the scale of G major requires that every F be played as F♯. Instead of writing a sharp in front of every F, a sharp is placed on the F line of the staff at the beginning of each line of music. This means that every F in the piece is played as F♯. If an F♮ is desired a natural sign is placed in front of that F.

The G Major Scale
(Using a one sharp key signature)

On the previous page you learned that the scale of D major requires sharps on the notes F and C. These, too, are placed in a key signature at the beginning of each staff.

The D Major Scale
(Using a two sharp key signature)

Since the key of C does not require any sharps, you may assume that the lack of a key signature indicates the key of C.

The C Major Scale
(No sharps or flats in key signature)

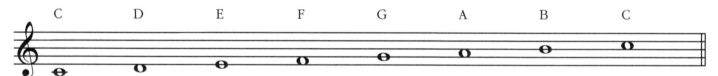

Summing Up

No Key Signature = Key of C

One-Sharp Key Signature = Key of G

Two-Sharp Key Signature = Key of D

Note: The above information does not necessarily apply to earlier material in this book which in some cases has been simplified to avoid using key signatures.

SCALE STUDIES

Scale studies are an important part of developing a fluent technique on the mandolin. The following studies should be played every day and each study should be approached in two stages:

1. Learning the Study

Play the study **very slowly.** Make sure that each note is correct and sounds clear. Check the fingering and picking for accuracy. Make sure that you're taking the key signature into account.

2. Practicing the Study

Once you can play the study slowly and accurately with good tone, start playing it a little faster each day. If you start making mistakes drop back to a slower tempo. A metronome is a great tool for measuring your progress. Remember: **It's better to play something beautifully and accurately at a slower tempo than to play it sloppily at a tempo that's too fast for you.** If you always practice accurately, the speed will come by itself.

THREE TUNES IN THREE KEYS

Rakes of Mallow (in G) Track 48

Irish fiddle tune

Tiritomba (in D) Track 49

Italian folk tune

Ain't Gonna Rain (in C) Track 50

American folk tune

 DYNAMICS

Music notation as we know it today made its greatest strides in 17th century Europe. Because Italians were pre-eminent at that time, many of the expressions we use in music are in that language.

Dynamics (how loud or soft to play) are based on three Italian words: *piano* (soft), *forte* (loud), and *mezzo* (moderately).

The most commonly used dynamics (from softest to loudest) are:

pp	*pianissimo*	=	very soft
p	*piano*	=	soft
mp	*mezzo piano*	=	moderately soft
mf	*mezzo forte*	=	moderately loud
f	*forte*	=	loud
ff	*fortissimo*	=	very loud

The dynamic mark applies to the note it is placed under and every succeeding note until a new dynamic mark is reached. Also commonly used is a temporary change in dynamics which only applies to the note under which it is found.

sfz (sforzando) = accented loud for that single note or chord, then soft

On mandolin, dynamics are produced by varying how you strike the strings. The harder you strike them the louder the tone.

Also important are the effects of gradually getting louder or softer. These are called (again in Italian):

crescendo (often abbreviated as ***cresc.***) = getting louder

*diminuendo** (abbreviated as ***dim.***) = getting softer

Another way of notating crescendos and diminuendos uses long, wedge-shaped marks familiarly known as "hairpins."

means to get louder

means to get softer

On the next page you'll find exercises and a song that make extensive use of dynamics.

Important: The proper use of dynamics is one of the things that distinguishes the artistic player from the ordinary player. Get in the habit of paying attention to the dynamics of a piece.

* A *diminuendo* is sometimes called *decrescendo*.

Exercise on Dynamics Track 51

Sippin' Cider Through a Straw Track 54

American folk song

DOTTED QUARTER NOTES

Placing a dot after a note increases its time value by half. For example, a half note gets two beats. Placing a dot after a half note increases its time value from two to three beats (2 + 1⁄2 of 2 = 3).

A dot after a quarter note also increases its value by half. Since a quarter note gets one beat, a dotted quarter gets 1-1⁄2 beats (1 + 1⁄2 of 1= 11⁄2). The next two staves show two different ways of notating this rhythm.

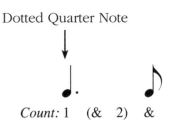

Dotted Quarter Note

Count: 1   (&   2)   &

Here are some familiar tunes that make prominent use of the dotted quarter note rhythm:

All Through the Night   Track 55

Welsh Christmas carol

Oh Susanna! Track 56

Stephen Foster

America Track 57

Old Saxon melody

CHORDS

A **chord** is a combination of two or more notes that sound good together. Chords are used to enhance a single-string melody making it sound richer and fuller. Chords can also be strummed to accompany the voice or another instrument, although because of the high pitch of the mandolin this technique is less effective than on the lower pitched guitar or banjo.

Unless they are whole notes, the notes of each chord have only one stem going either up or down. This means that the notes of the chord are struck together to produce one sound. Here are some examples of how chords are written for the mandolin: (not to be played)

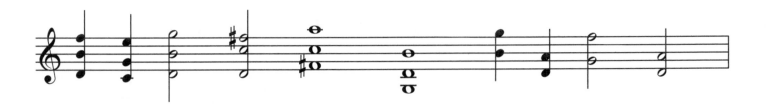

Preliminary Study Track 58

In this study the notes of some two-string chords (also called **intervals**) are played separately, then together. Make sure the two-note chords sound as one. Your pick stroke must be quick and accurate.

Hint: Read chords from the top down, not from the bottom up. Once the top note is in place, the rest of the chord follows naturally.

Three-Note Chords (in the key of G) Track 59

Here are some melodies that use two- and three-note chords:

Plaisir d'amour (The Joys of Love) Track 60

G. Martini

Ode to Joy (Theme from Symphony No. 9) Track 61

Ludwig van Beethoven

Reminder: Don't forget to practice your tremolo technique every day.

 TEMPO

Tempo is a word of Italian origin used to indicate how fast a piece of music is to be played. In classical music, tempo indications are usually in Italian.

The most commonly used, from the slowest to the fastest tempo, are:

grave	=	very slow; the slowest tempo used in music
largo	=	slow and broad
lento	=	slowly
adagio	=	slow, but not as slow as *lento*
andante	=	moderately slow
moderato	=	moderately fast
allegro	=	fast
presto	=	very fast
presstissimo	=	as fast as possible

Since these are not exact indications, personal taste plays an important role in choosing the right tempo.

Popular arrangers and bluegrass musicians tend to use plain English such as **moderately fast, bright, with a lilt** and so on.

Metronome markings are the most definite way of indicating tempo. At the beginning of a piece you may see ♩ = 120. This means that quarter notes are to be played at 120 beats per minute. If you own a metronome just set it at 120 and use the clicks you hear for the basic beat.

A few other expressions refer to changes of tempo:

accel. is the abbreviation for *accelerando* = getting faster

rit. is the abbreviation for *ritardando* = held back, slower

rall. is the abbreviation for *rallentando* = slowing down

stretto = hurrying

When a tempo that has been altered reverts to the original tempo, the Italian expression *a tempo* is used.

This beautiful melody was adapted for the 1953 Broadway musical Kismet where it was called "Stranger in Paradise."

KEY SIGNATURES WITH FLATS

A piece of music based on the F major scale is said to be "in F." The key signature for F major is one flat. That flat is B. This means that every B in the key of F is played as B♭ unless preceded by a natural sign.

The F Major Scale
(Using a one-flat key signature)

A piece of music based on the B♭ major scale is said to be "in B♭." The key signature for the key of B♭ is two flats, B and E. This means that every B is played as B♭, and that every E is played as E♭ unless preceded by a natural sign.

The B♭ Major Scale
(Using a two-flat key signature)

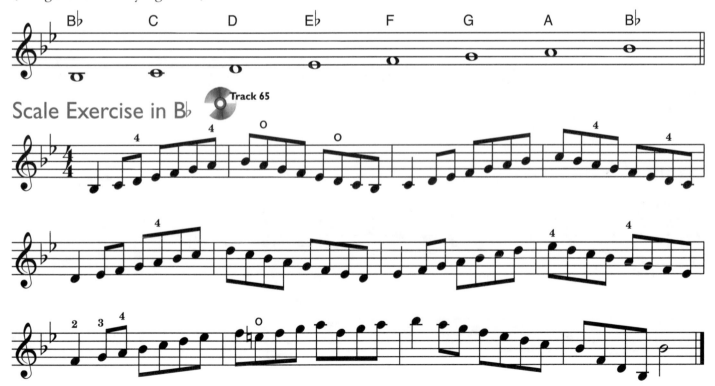

TWO SONGS IN TWO KEYS

These pieces are in $\frac{2}{4}$ time, which means there are two beats in each measure.

Melodie (in F) Track 66

Anton Rubinstein

MINI MUSIC LESSON EIGHTH RESTS ❼

The symbol ❼ is used to indicate an eighth rest.
This symbol means to leave a silence the length of an eighth note, that is, a half beat.

When eighth notes appear alone, they look like ♪ or ♩.

Single eighth notes are often used with eighth rests: ♪ ❼ ♪ ❼
Count: 1 & 2 &

Eighth rests are also used with beamed eighth notes: ❼ ♫ ❼

Play the following rhythm on open strings:

Count: 1 & 2 & 3 & 4 &   1 & 2 & 3 & 4 &

When playing open strings the sound is cut off by lightly placing the heel of the right hand against the strings to stop their vibration. You must do this for each rest.

When playing fingered notes the sound is cut off by releasing the pressure on the string, but keeping the finger in light contact with it.

Eighth rests may also appear on downbeats. This creates no unusual problem if the player **marks the downbeat by tapping the foot or counting mentally.**

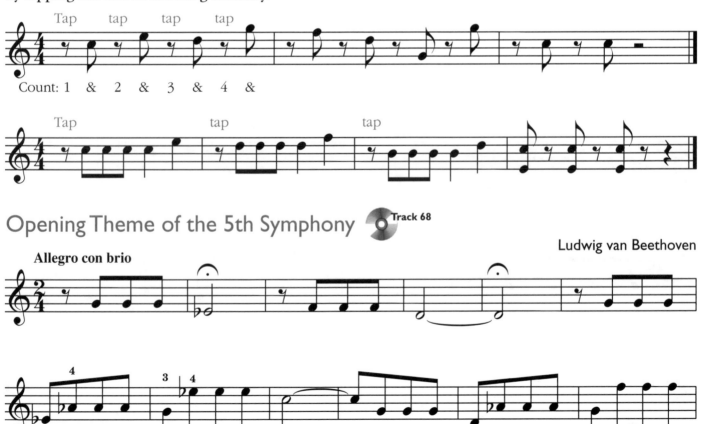

Opening Theme of the 5th Symphony 🎵 Track 68

Ludwig van Beethoven

Allegro con brio

La Bamba Track 69

Latin-American folk song

Allegro moderato

Note: the measures between the repeat signs ‖: :‖ are usually played twice. If it's marked "repeat and fade," then the player keeps repeating the passage, gradually fading, until it's no longer heard.

 ## $\frac{6}{8}$ TIME

The "8" in the $\frac{6}{8}$ time signature means that each eighth note now gets one full beat (unlike $\frac{2}{4}$, $\frac{3}{4}$ and $\frac{4}{4}$, where the quarter note equals one beat). The "6" means that there are six beats per measure. Songs which are played in a slow to moderately slow tempo are counted "in six," that is, with six full beats per measure.

Track 70

Slow to moderate

Count: 1 2 3 4 5 6   1 2 3 4 5 6   1 2 3 4 5 6   1 2 3 4 5 6

The next two songs are typical melodies in slow $\frac{6}{8}$ time. Count them in six.

Drink to Me Only with Thine Eyes   Track 71

Anonymous

Un Canadien Errant (A Wandering Canadian)   Track 72

Words by Antoine Gérain-Lajoie

Music: Anonymous

MINI MUSIC LESSON $\frac{6}{8}$ TIME (Part II)

When the tempo of $\frac{6}{8}$ time is faster, it becomes difficult to count in six. Any tempo faster than moderate should be counted "in two." This means that each measure will contain two beats; Each beat will contain three eighth notes.

 Track 73

This familiar children's song is an example of $\frac{6}{8}$ time counted in two:

The Farmer in the Dell   Track 74

Fast $\frac{6}{8}$ time is also characteristic of Irish jigs.

The Irish Washerwoman   Track 75

* Bring 1st finger up to the 3rd fret

16TH NOTES

A 16th note looks like ♪ or 𝅘𝅥𝅯 when it stands alone. When they are written in groups of two or more, 16th notes look like this:

A 16th note is played twice as quickly as an eighth note and four times as quickly as a quarter note. In $\frac{2}{4}$, $\frac{3}{4}$ and $\frac{4}{4}$ times there are four 16th notes in each beat. Count them as 1 e & uh, 2 e & uh, etc.

Always play 16th notes with alternating down- and upstrokes of the pick.

Make sure you can play the exercises on this page before attempting the tunes that follow.

The Drunken Sailor — Track 76

Allegro

Traditional sea chantey

Count: 1 & uh 2 & uh   1 & 2 &

1 & 2 &

Cripple Creek — Track 77

Moderato

Traditional folk tune

Count: 1 & uh 2 e &   1 e & 2 &   1 & uh 2 e & uh   1 e & uh 2 &

Old Aunt Jenny — Track 78

Moderato

Traditional

* Play *p* first time through and *f* on the repeat.

THE DOTTED EIGHTH & 16TH NOTE RHYTHM

Like a group of two eighth notes, the dotted eighth and 16th rhythm takes one beat to play. However, unlike eighth notes (which are played evenly) dotted eighth and 16ths are played unevenly: long short, long short.

Compare the following:

Eighth notes:

Count: 1 & 2 & 3 & 4 & 1 & 2 & 3 & 4 &

Dotted eighth, and 16ths:

Count: 1 e & uh 2 e & uh 3 e & uh 4 e & uh 1 e & uh 2 e & uh 3 e & uh 4 e & uh

Or, you can think of this rhythm by remembering the sound of the words: "Hump - ty Dump - ty, Hump - ty Dump - ty"

The dotted eighth and 16th note rhythm is common in all styles of music. Here are examples of each to practice.

Toreador Song (from the opera *Carmen*)   Track 79

Georges Bizet

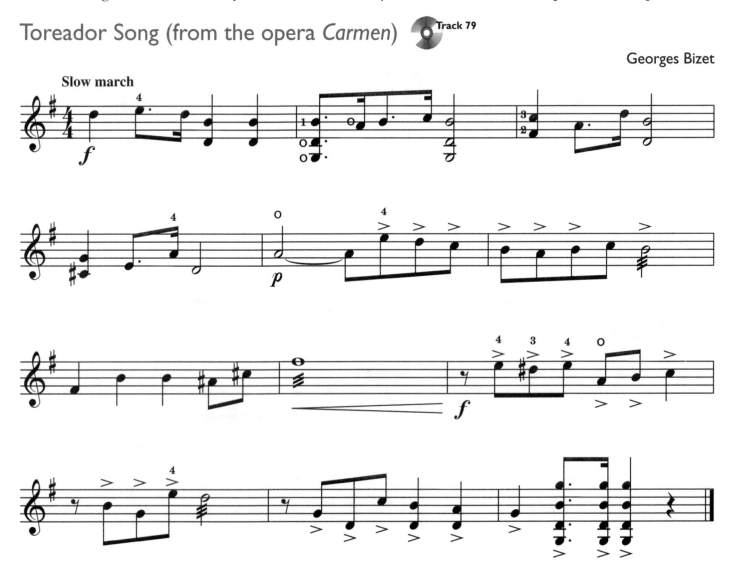

Note: The symbol > is called an accent. It means to play that note stronger (harder) than usual.

Straight Jig

Track 80

Irish folk tune

Count: 1 uh 2 uh 3 & 4 &

Put Your Little Foot

Track 81

Country waltz

E sharp is the same as F natural (1st string, 1st fret)

Boogie Blues

Track 82

THE DOTTED EIGHTH & 16TH NOTE RHYTHM (continued)

In $\frac{6}{8}$ time, the dotted eighth and 16th note rhythm is played like the dotted quarter and eighth note rhythm in $\frac{2}{4}$, $\frac{3}{4}$ or $\frac{4}{4}$. Count carefully.

Andante cantabile means "moderately fast in a singing manner."

CROSSPICKING

Crosspicking refers to picking that moves from string to string. It's one of the harder things to do on the mandolin, but is a wonderful effect when you master it. Here are two old fiddle tunes that require a lot of crosspicking. Learn them at a very slow tempo paying great attention to details such as fingering, picking, and of course, tone. Once you have mastered the basics, start increasing the tempo gradually till you can play it at about ♩ = 80 to 100.

Soldier's Joy
Track 85
Traditional

Cincinnati Hornpipe
Track 86
Traditional

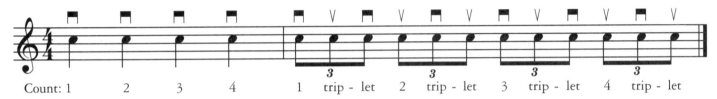

THE EIGHTH NOTE TRIPLET

An **eighth-note triplet** is a group of three eighth notes played in one beat. You'll recognize the triplet by the number 3 over the three eighth notes. First practice the exercises, then play the song.

Using the triplet in various meters:

Amazing Grace   Track 87

American folk hymn

This old fragment is a good way to remember the sound of a triplet.

Shave and a Haircut Track 88

1st AND 2nd ENDINGS

You have already learned that music between repeat signs ‖: :‖ is played twice. Sometimes an entire section is repeated except for the last few measures. In a case like this, **1st and 2nd endings** are used.

1st and 2nd endings are used in this arrangement of a famous Italian melody. Play the first 16 measures. Then, repeat the first 14 measures, skip the two measures under the ⌐1. and play the two measures under the ⌐2. instead.

Serenade (from the ballet *Harlequin's Millions*) Track 89

Riccardo Drigo

*__Allegretto cantabile__ means moderately fast (but slower than **allegro**) and in a singing manner.

** This note is high C. It is played on the 1st string, 8th fret.

Tremolo Study No. 2

Start at about ♩ = 80. Work your way up to ♩ = 160. Keep the right wrist slightly curved and relaxed. Strive for a smooth, even tone.

The use of tremolo can be extended to cover entire phrases. This is particularly effective in sentimental melodies such as this famous Italian waltz. Only the eighths, are played as individual notes. The long curved lines are called **phrase marks** (not to be confused with **ties**). Do not interrupt the tremolo within the phrase.

Fascination — Track 90

F. D. Marchetti

Remember that when playing tremolo on a chord, it generally sounds better to tremolo only the highest note while sustaining the others.

OTHER TIME SIGNATURES ($\frac{3}{8}$ and $\frac{9}{8}$)

Each measure of $\frac{3}{8}$ **time** is played like a half measure of $\frac{6}{8}$. That is, there are three beats per measure, and the eighth note gets the beat.

Old Rosin the Bow

Track 91

American folk song

$\frac{9}{8}$ **time** can be thought of as three measures of $\frac{3}{8}$, or as a measure of $\frac{6}{8}$ followed by one measure of $\frac{3}{8}$. Although not often seen, $\frac{9}{8}$ has been used for "The Impossible Dream," "Send in the Clowns," and this famous melody.

Beautiful Dreamer

Track 92

Stephen Foster

THE KEY OF D MINOR

Every major key shares a key signature with a **relative minor key**. For example, both the key of F major and the key of D minor share a key signature of one flat. Practice the scale of D minor, and then play what may be the most famous Italian song ever written.

Notice that the song uses both the key of D minor (one flat) and the key of D major (two sharps). Use tremolo at your own discretion.

Scale Study in D Minor   Track 93

Torna a Surriento (Come Back to Sorrento)   Track 94

Ernesto de Curtis

COMMON TIME AND CUT TIME

The symbol $\mathbf{C}$ used as a time signature is another way of saying $\frac{4}{4}$ time.

The symbol $\mathbf{\mathct{C}}$ calls for "cut time." It means to play the same number of notes per measure as $\frac{4}{4}$, but to count only two beats to each measure. This is especially useful when the tempo gets fast enough to make counting four beats to the measure awkward. Cut time is used for fast show tunes, marches and other music meant to be played brightly. Play this famous march in cut time. Count as indicated, and keep the tempo bright ($\frac{1}{2}$ =96–120).

The Stars and Stripes Forever   Track 95

John Philip Sousa

CHORDS

In bluegrass bands and some rock and alternative rock bands, the mandolin is sometimes required to strum chords. A **chord** is a group of three or more notes that sound good together. Chords have names consisting of two parts:

• The first part names the note upon which the chord is based such as A, B♭, F♯ and so on. This note is called the root of the chord.

• The second part of the chord is called the **suffix**. It tells you what kind of a chord it is. Suffixes are usually abbreviated such as m for minor, 7 for seventh, a small circle for diminished and so on.

A **chord symbol** such as A7 tells you that the root of the chord is A and that it is a seventh chord. Every chord symbol has a suffix except for major chords which use only the root. Thus, C means a C major chord; F♯ means an F♯ major chord and so on. The chart below shows you the names and abbreviations of the most common chords. A basic chord dictionary including fingering diagrams may be found on pages 66–71.

Suffix	Type of chord
(none)	major
m or min	minor
7	seventh (sometimes called dominant seventh)
° or dim	diminished
+ or aug	augmented
m7 or min 7	minor seventh
m6 or min 6	minor sixth
maj7, M7 or Δ	major seventh
6 or maj 6	major sixth
min/maj7 or m+7	minor major seventh

Certain notes in the chords may be altered such as

-5 or ♭5	lower the 5th of the chord 1/2 step (one fret)
+5 or ♯5	raise the 5th of the chord 1/2 step (one fret)
-9 or ♭9	lower the 9th of the chord 1/2 step (one fret)
+9 or ♯9	raise the 9th of the chord 1/2 step (one fret)
sus4	raise the 3rd of the chord 1/2 step (one fret)

For the casual player there's really no need to understand the theory behind the construction of chords. My suggestion is to memorize the basic chord diagrams on the following pages, and strum them when the occasion calls for it. Those who are serious about their musical studies should get a book on music theory such as *Alfred's Teach Yourself Guitar Theory* by Roger Edison. Although written for guitar, this book contains much valuable information which will be understandable to the average mandolinist.

MANDOLIN ACCOMPANIMENTS

Accompaniment patterns, often called strums, are played by striking the pick rapidly across the strings so that all the notes in the chord sound together.

 = strum the strings (use any chord) ■ = strum *down* across the strings V = strum *up* across the strings > = accent or give emphasis

Ballad
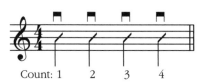
Count: 1   2   3   4

Country-Shuffle
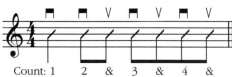
Count: 1 da 2 da 3 da 4 da

Basic Rock

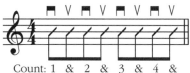
Count: 1 & 2 & 3 & 4 &

Dixieland

Count: 1   2   3   4

Nashville

Count: 1   2 & 3 & 4 &

Tango or Habanera
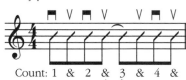
Count: 1 & 2 & 3   4

Rhumba
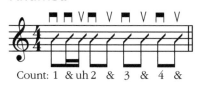
Count: 1 & uh 2 & 3 & 4 &

'50s fast rock 'n' roll
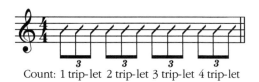
Count: 1   2 & 3 & 4

Calypso

Count: 1 & 2 & 3 & 4 &

Ragtime
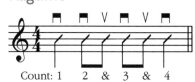
Count: 1   2 & 3 & 4

'50s slow rock 'n' roll
Count: 1 trip-let 2 trip-let 3 trip-let 4 trip-let

Country Waltz

Count: 1   2   3

Bluegrass

Count: 1   2 & 3   4 &

Blues
Count: 1 uh 2 uh 3 uh 4 uh

Country Waltz Variation
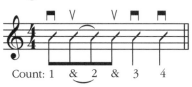
Count: 1   2 & 3

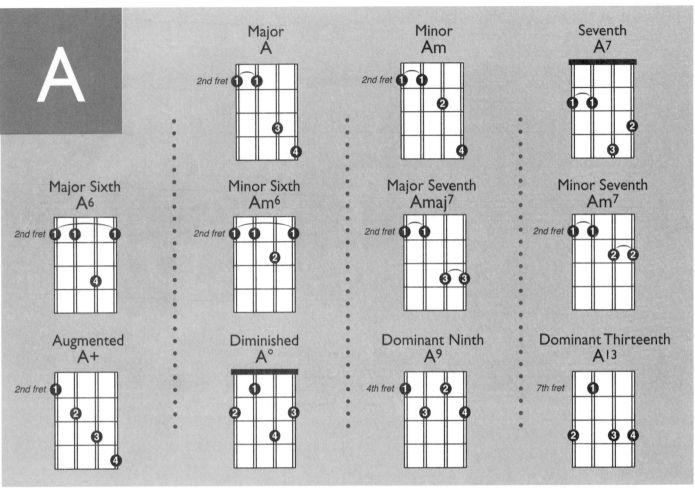

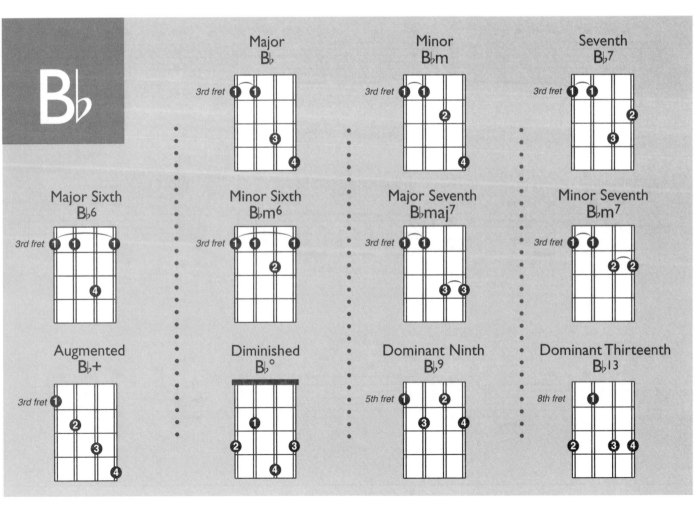

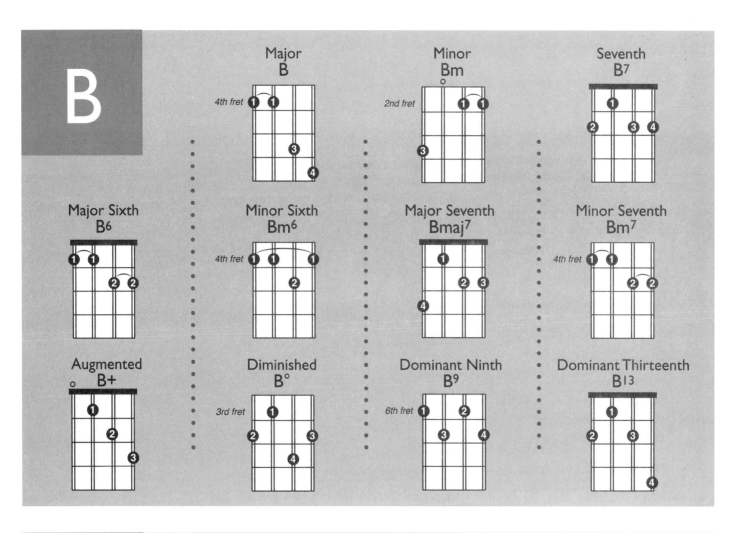

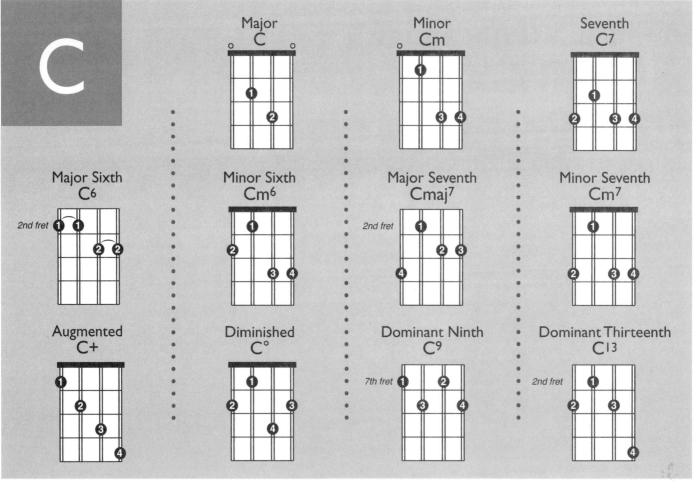

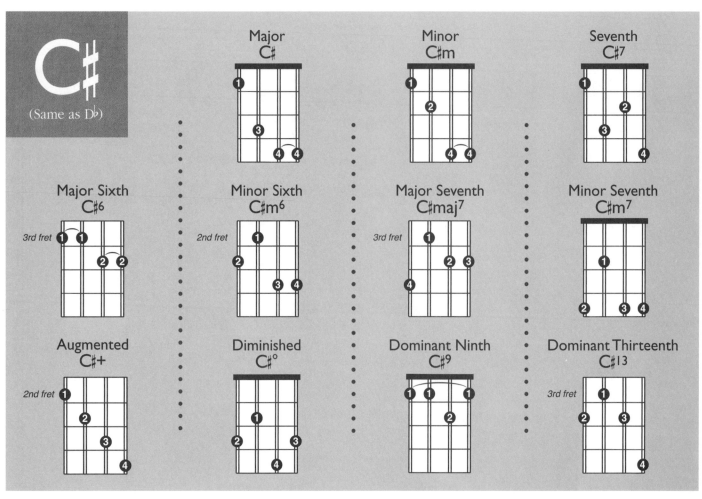

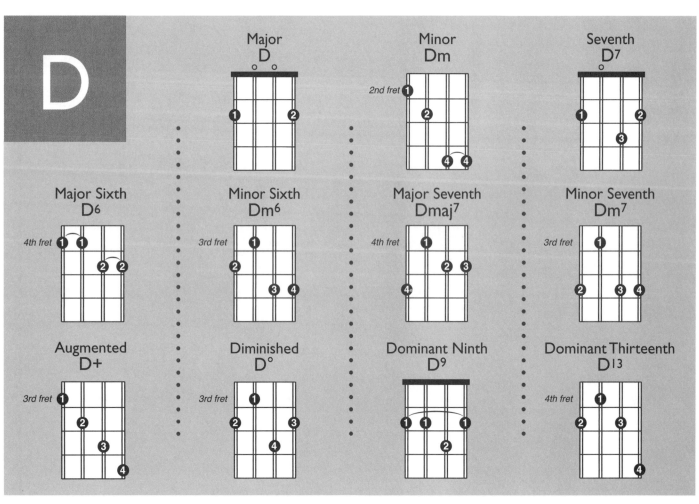

Mandolin Chord Dictionary

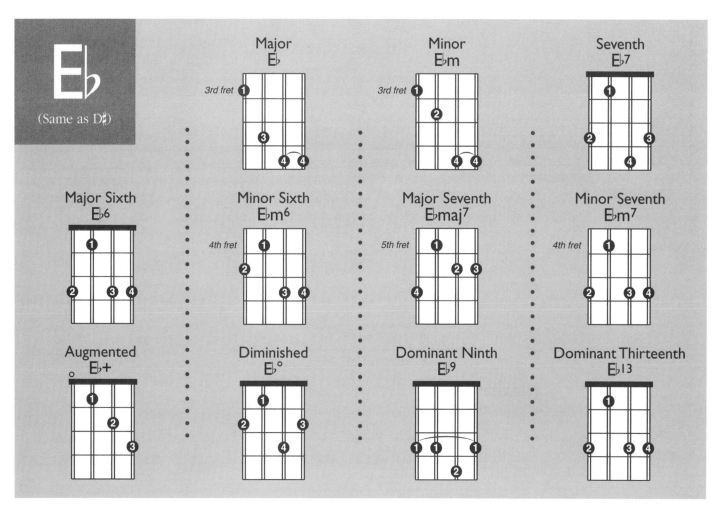

Eb
(Same as D#)

Major
Eb

Minor
Ebm

Seventh
Eb7

Major Sixth
Eb6

Minor Sixth
Ebm6

Major Seventh
Ebmaj7

Minor Seventh
Ebm7

Augmented
Eb+

Diminished
Eb°

Dominant Ninth
Eb9

Dominant Thirteenth
Eb13

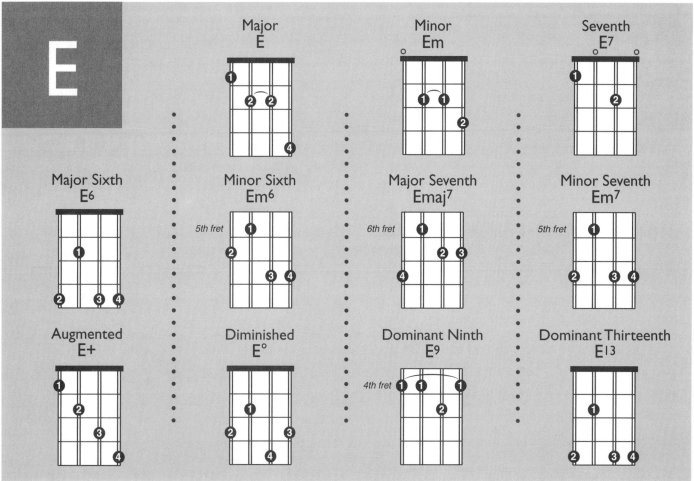

E

Major
E

Minor
Em

Seventh
E7

Major Sixth
E6

Minor Sixth
Em6

Major Seventh
Emaj7

Minor Seventh
Em7

Augmented
E+

Diminished
E°

Dominant Ninth
E9

Dominant Thirteenth
E13

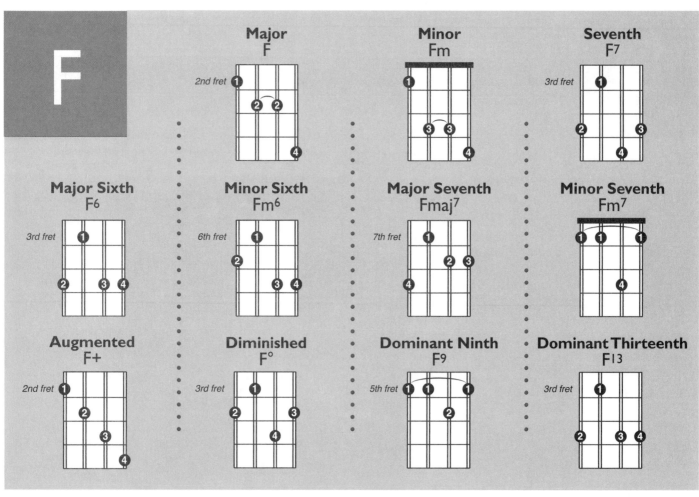

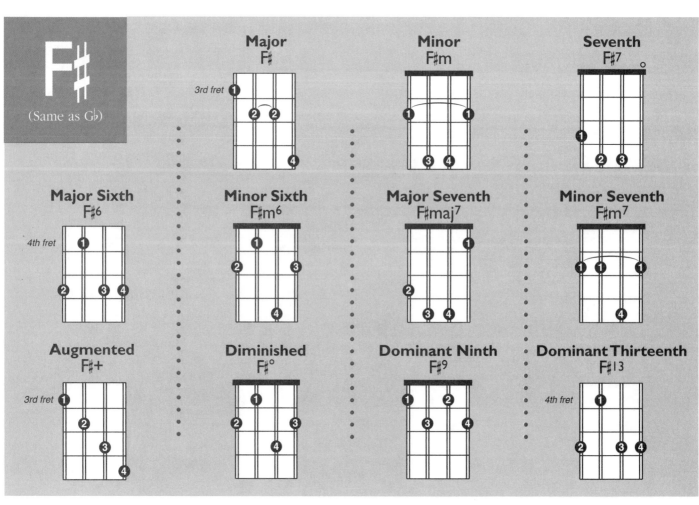

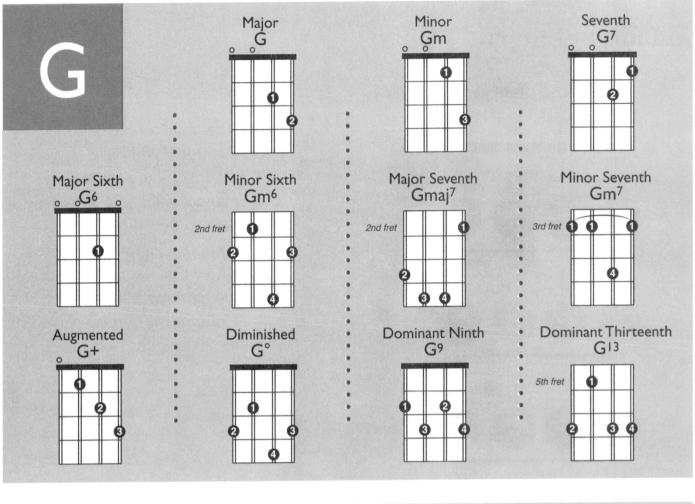

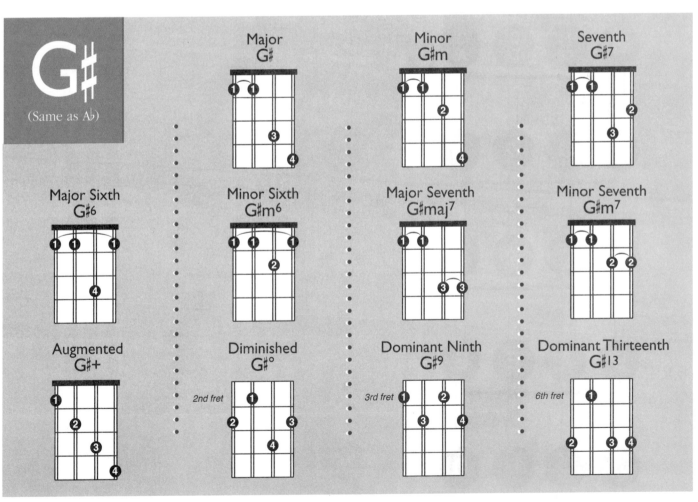

Mandolin Fingering Chart

The first position

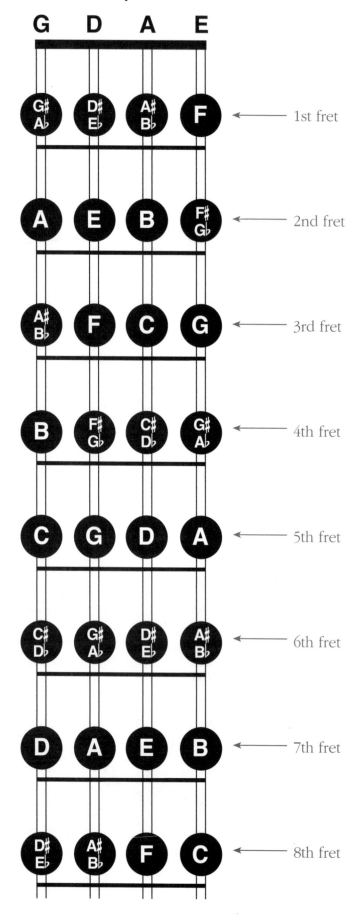

Now that you've completed this book you have a good understanding of basic mandolin technique. Now it's time to find other music in your special field of interest. Know that except for music in the extreme high register, any violin music can be played on the mandolin. Good luck!